BLOODY MARY

GHOST OF A QUEEN?

─◆─ BY AUBRE ANDRUS ◆─

CAPSTONE PRESS
a capstone imprint

Snap Books are published by Capstone Press
1710 Roe Crest Drive, North Mankato, Minnesota 56003
www.capstonepub.com

Library of Congress Cataloging-in-Publication Data
Names: Andrus, Aubre, author.
Title: Bloody Mary : ghost of a queen? / by Aubre Andrus.
Description: North Mankato, Minnesota : Capstone Press, 2019. | Series: Snap:
real-life ghost stories | Includes bibliographical references and index.
Identifiers: LCCN 2018059096| ISBN 9781543573367 (hardcover) | ISBN
9781543574784 (pbk.) | ISBN 9781543573459 (ebook pdf)
Subjects: LCSH: Bloody Mary (Legendary character)—Juvenile literature.
Classification: LCC GR75.B56 A64 2019 | DDC 398.2—dc23
LC record available at https://lccn.loc.gov/2018059096

Editorial Credits
Eliza Leahy, editor; Brann Garvey, designer; Tracy Cummins, media researcher;
Tori Abraham, production specialist

Photo Credits
Alamy: De Luan, 8, PRISMA ARCHIVO, 7; Bridgeman Images: Private Collection/PVDE,
15; Getty Images: Kaz Chiba, 27; Shutterstock: Aleshyn_Andrei, 4, Anna Kogut, 24,
Anne Greenwood, 19, avtk, Design Element, Chantal de Bruijne, Design Element,
ChiccoDodiFC, 20, Chinnapong (ribbon), 23, Dale A Stork, 12, Dragana Djorovic, 11,
Giraphics, Design Element, GoMixer, Design Element, Igor Sokolov (scissors), 23,
igorstevanovic (bible), 23, Joe Techapanupreeda, Cover, MagicDogWorkshop, Design
Element, NikhomTreeVector, Design Element, NinaMalyna (frame), 7, PeterVrabel,
16-17, Prokrida (frame), 5, 13 Bottom, 13 Top, 21 Bottom, 21 Top

Printed in the United States of America.
PA70

TABLE OF CONTENTS

THE LEGEND OF BLOODY MARY

The bathroom is dark, and the door is closed. The only noise is your breath, slow and steady. A flickering candle casts a soft glow on your face. You stare into the mirror and begin whispering, "Bloody Mary, Bloody Mary, Bloody Mary . . ."

This **ritual** has been a popular—and scary!—slumber party game in the United States since the 1970s. It's a fear test that only the brave dare play. Why? Because if you believe the legend, chanting "Bloody Mary" in front of a mirror will **summon** an angry spirit.

Those who've played this game claim to see the reflection of a woman. But what she looks like and what happens next is up for debate. Some say she's an evil witch. Others claim to see a **gruesome** corpse. Some viewers see red tears drip down her face, or a dead baby in her arms. She may scream, curse, or even reach out of the mirror to scratch your face bloody with her long fingernails.

Skeptics think that sightings of Bloody Mary could be explained by people's eyes playing tricks on them. But legend says this terrifying spirit steals the souls of those who call upon her. Anyone who plays the game could be strangled, trapped in the mirror, or haunted by Bloody Mary's ghost forever.

MYSTERY OF MIRRORS

The ancient Romans believed a person's reflection was their soul. Breaking a mirror meant your soul would be damaged for seven years. They weren't the only ones who believed this. Some cultures believe that covering mirrors with a sheet after someone dies can help the deceased person's soul move on to the **afterworld**. Other cultures believe in covering mirrors every night before they go to sleep. And some believe they shouldn't look in a mirror at night for fear they will get sick or die.

CHAPTER ONE

BLOODY MARY IN REAL LIFE

Nobody knows for sure who Bloody Mary was or why she **allegedly** appears in the reflections of mirrors around the world. There are many different people whom the legend of Bloody Mary could be based on, including English royalty, an accused witch, and an evil murderer. Depending on which version you believe, there are different ways to summon her and different reasons she appears.

SKEPTIC'S NOTE

People disagree as to how many times Bloody Mary should be repeated—anywhere from three to one hundred times. And others disagree on exactly what to say. Some versions of the tale repeat longer phrases, such as, "Bloody Mary, I have your baby." Still others perform various actions such as flushing the toilet, blowing out a candle, or spinning around three times.

Mary Tudor ruled England from 1553–1558. Her reign was marked by her **persecution** of Protestants.

QUEEN MARY I

Are you brave enough to chant the phrases "Bloody Mary, I stole your baby" or "Bloody Mary, I killed your baby"? The image that appears in the mirror is often said to be the ghost of Queen Mary I. Legend says that she is unhappily searching for a missing child.

Thomas Cranmer was a leader of the Protestants. He was burned alive during Queen Mary I's reign.

Mary Tudor became the first queen of England in 1553. Although she only ruled for five years, she was a queen no one could forget. She believed that everyone should follow her religion, Roman Catholicism. Those who didn't were burned alive. They were known as Protestants. Hundreds of people fled the country to save themselves. But nearly three hundred men, women, and children were captured and killed while Queen Mary I was in charge. The people of England couldn't believe their queen could act so cruelly. They gave her a nickname: Bloody Mary.

During this time, Queen Mary I was believed to be pregnant twice. She looked pregnant and felt pregnant. But each time, a baby was never born. Afterward, she never mentioned the pregnancies again. She died childless. Now legend says that her angry ghost haunts the mirrors of children who call to her. She wants to reach through the mirror and capture them.

FACT

Today it is believed that Queen Mary I suffered from false pregnancies. False pregnancy is when a woman believes so strongly that she is pregnant that her body starts changing as if she really was.

MARY WORTH

Some who play the Bloody Mary game chant the phrase, "I believe in Mary Worth," while holding a single candle. According to local legend, Mary Worth was a witch. She lived on a farm near Chicago, Illinois, around the time of the Civil War.

At that time, many **enslaved** people tried to escape from the South to the North on a secret network of helpful people called the Underground Railroad. Many people believe that instead of providing safety to those who were seeking freedom, Mary Worth captured them. She is said to have performed evil spells on her **victims**. She would **torture** them and eventually kill them. It wasn't long before people found out what she was doing. Legend says they put an end to her dark magic by burning her alive.

FACT

Some who call upon Bloody Mary Worth claim to see their shower curtains go up in flames . . . even though their candles were far away.

Years later, a farmer and his wife built a house right on top of the remains of Mary's barn. While farming in the field, the man found a large stone. He moved it to his front yard. Then strange things started happening. His wife got locked in the house. Plates crashed to the floor. The farmer wondered if the stone he moved was from Mary's gravesite. He tried to put the stone back but could never find the right spot.

According to the legend, the hauntings continued. Years later the house burned to the ground. Since then, no one has been able to build on that property. Anytime something is built near Mary Worth's barn, it burns to the ground.

There's no historical data that proves Mary Worth existed during the time of the Civil War and the Underground Railroad. Even so, her story has become local legend in the Chicago area and continues to be told.

ANOTHER MARY WORTH

Others believe Mary Worth was a vain woman who was killed in a car accident. She suffered severe injuries to her face. People say she appears as an angry spirit in mirrors to **avenge** her death and bring suffering to others.

ELIZABETH BÁTHORY

Even though her name isn't Mary, Countess Elizabeth Báthory may have inspired the Bloody Mary legend. She loved looking in mirrors, and she really loved blood—the blood of young girls in particular.

Elizabeth Báthory ruled from her castle in Slovakia in the sixteenth and early seventeenth centuries. During this time, young girls in town kept disappearing. No one knew why. But Elizabeth had a plan. She was obsessed with looking young. Legend says that she believed she could look even more beautiful if she killed young women and bathed in their blood.

Elizabeth started killing castle servants. When there were no more young girls to capture in the castle, she asked the castle guards to kidnap local peasant girls and bring them to her.

SKEPTIC'S NOTE

While Elizabeth Báthory was a proven serial killer, there is no historical proof that she bathed in her victims' blood. It is simply a local legend.

ITISSA ELISABETHA BATHORI
TIS FRANCISCI DE NADASD FILII
TIS THOMAE DE NADASD PALATINI
AE CONIVX. ANNO MDLXXXIV.

Elizabeth Báthory was born into a powerful Hungarian family in 1560.

15

Elizabeth Báthory lived in the castle Hrad Cachtice. The ruins are located in what is now Slovakia.

Elizabeth continued to kill and torture girls. As the years went on, she grew careless. People soon discovered the dead bodies of young women in her castle, Hrad Cachtice. In just six years, she had tortured and killed up to 650 girls. Elizabeth became known as the Blood Countess.

Because she was a **noblewoman**, Elizabeth couldn't be put on trial or sentenced to death. Instead, a brick wall was built in front of her bedroom door to imprison her within her own castle. A few years later, she was found dead. Elizabeth Báthory now holds the Guinness World Record as the Most **Prolific** Female Murderer.

Some people who call to Elizabeth's ghost claim to find their faces instantly covered in dripping blood. When they wipe it off, hundreds of scratches mysteriously cover their face.

FACT

Elizabeth Báthory was also called Countess Dracula.

CHAPTER TWO

BLOODY MARY AROUND THE WORLD

The Bloody Mary tradition is a modern ghost story that has now traveled worldwide thanks to the internet and websites like YouTube. Now kids all over the world repeat the scary phrase in front of their mirrors. Depending on where you live in the world, the ghost's name, and how you call to her, what happens afterward can vary.

SVARTA MADAME

In Sweden, kids summon Svarta Madame, the "black woman." There are a couple different ways to call for her. Some children chant, "I don't believe in you, Svarta Madame," twelve times while standing in front of a mirror in a dark room. Others say, "Black Madame, Black Madame. Daughter of the Devil, show yourself." Then they splash water on the mirror. The woman who appears in the reflection always looks the same: glowing yellow eyes, red teeth, black skin, and green hair.

What happens next could be good or bad. You could instantly die. Or the ghost could bring you bad luck. Or possibly good fortune! This legend is so popular in Sweden that there's even been a movie made about it.

HANAKO-SAN

School bathrooms are one of the few places where adults are not watching children, so it's a great place to play a game like Bloody Mary. That may be why a ghostly figure is said to haunt school bathrooms in Japan. Japanese kids claim to hear voices, see doors slam, and watch lights flicker when they're alone in a bathroom.

Daring souls try to summon the ghost in person. They stand close to the door of the third bathroom stall and knock three times while asking, "Are you there, Hanako-san?" People have claimed to see a hand burst through the door. Legend says that the unfamiliar hand will grab the person and kill them. Others say the ghost answers, "Yes, I'm here," or the door will open a bit by itself. Inside the stall, a girlish ghost wearing an old-fashioned red dress is believed to appear.

FLUSH!

Despite the differences, the Bloody Mary tale always has ties to bathrooms, probably because they are small, dark, and have a mirror. You can easily shut off the lights, close the door, and have a little privacy while you play the Bloody Mary game. Some U.S. versions of the Bloody Mary tale go so far as to flush the toilet as part of the ritual. Sometimes the flush is needed to summon the ghost. Other times a push of the lever turns the water in the toilet red.

The ghost girl is named Toire no Hanako-san, which means, "Hanako of the Toilet." Some believe she's the spirit of a young girl who died during World War II. Local legend says that while she was playing hide-and-seek in the bathroom stall, a plane bombed the school. The building collapsed on top of her. Others believe she was a victim of bullying who hid in the third stall and was later found dead. Maybe that's why her ghost is believed to protect kids who are getting bullied.

VERONICA

In Spain and Mexico, kids tell a similar Bloody Mary story called Nueve Veces Veronica, or Nine Times Veronica. She's believed to be the spirit of a young girl who died while trying to call upon ghosts using a Bible, a red ribbon, and scissors. The legend says that Veronica and her friends were summoning ghosts in an abandoned house. Veronica didn't take it seriously, which made the ghosts mad. Before her friends could react, the scissors allegedly flew through the air, stabbing Veronica in the neck. She died immediately.

Those who are brave enough to call for Veronica's ghost light a candle in front of the mirror in a dark room just before midnight. Then, at exactly midnight, they repeat, "Veronica," nine times. Most importantly, they never laugh or make a joke, so as not to anger Veronica. People say that when she appears, the ghost is seen gripping the bloody scissors in her hands.

Some believe Veronica can answer questions about life or death. Others say she will stab you with her scissors. Still others think that nothing will happen right away, but days later your mirror may fog up with a message that reads, *I am Veronica*. She will quietly haunt your house forever. Believers say there's no way to ever get rid of her.

FACT

When a ghost appears in a physical, humanlike form that can be seen—as opposed to a cold burst of air or a spooky feeling or event—it's called an **apparition**.

CHAPTER THREE

DO YOU SEE WHAT I SEE?

Mirrors appear in legends all around the world. Historically, they have been seen as paths to another world, like in *Alice's Adventures in Wonderland* when Alice passes through the looking glass. In literature and art, mirrors are also often used as a way of communicating with spirits. An example of this is in *Snow White* when the evil queen talks to a ghostly face in the mirror. So it's no surprise that the Bloody Mary legend has spread far and wide, despite the mysteries surrounding it.

FACT

When using a mirror to summon a ghost, it's called **enoptromancy**.

While there are many versions of the Bloody Mary ritual, these parts remain the same: a mirror, a darkened room, and a phrase that's chanted a certain number of times. And, of course, a frightening female figure. But no one knows who this woman is or why she appears. There's no agreement on exactly what she looks like or what she will do once you're standing face-to-face with her. And that might be exactly why kids want to meet her. Many brush off the Bloody Mary legend as a simple "fear test" that lets someone try something scary in a safe place. Or is it really true?

Some people get a thrill out of summoning spirits. The expectation that something will happen is sometimes enough to make us think we saw something. That could be why the legend of Bloody Mary is still passed around to kids all over the world today. As we hear the story over and over again, we begin to believe it. But are you brave enough to say it? *Bloody Mary . . . Bloody Mary . . . Bloody Mary . . .*

SKEPTIC'S NOTE

After squinting in the darkness for a few minutes, your eyes can easily play tricks on your mind. When playing Bloody Mary, staring at your own reflection while reciting her name could be enough to trick your eyes and mind that you've seen a ghost. It could be a **hallucination**—when you think you see or hear something even if it's not there—or it could be a simple optical **illusion**.

Try staring at your own reflection in the mirror. In less than a minute, you'll see your face start changing shape. Keep staring and it will become distorted and scary looking. It might even look like an angry spirit! It turns out that if you stare at something long enough, your brain will fade out the details around it. They'll begin to blend into the background. It's called the **Troxler Effect**.

Stare at the red dot for twenty seconds and see what happens. More than likely, the blue circle surrounding it will start to gradually fade into the background and eventually disappear. This is just one example of this optical illusion in action.

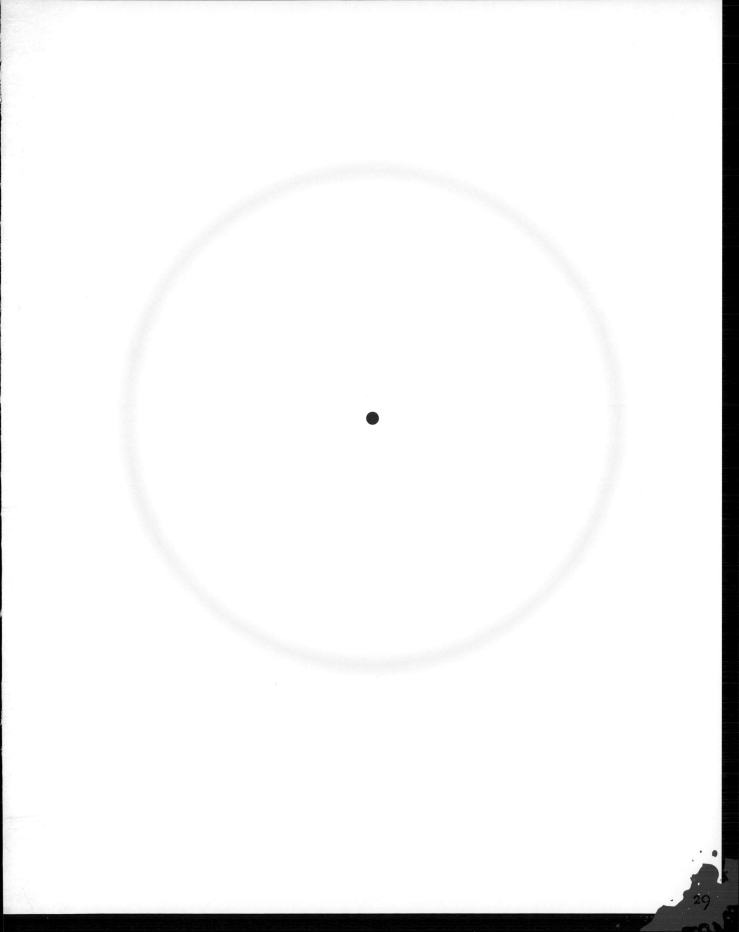

GLOSSARY

afterworld (AF-tur-wurld)—a place where beings go after they die

allegedly (uh-LEDGE-id-lee)—said to be true or to have happened, but without proof

apparition (ap-uh-RISH-uhn)—an unexpected sight or a ghostly image of a person

avenge (uh-VENJ)—to punish someone who has harmed you

enoptromancy (en-OP-troh-mehn-see)—using a mirror to summon a ghost

enslaved (in-SLAYVED)—a person who is enslaved is forced to be the legal property of another person and to obey him or her

gruesome (GROO-suhm)—very unpleasant, disgusting, or horrible

hallucination (huh-loo-sih-NAY-shuhn)—an experience of seeing or hearing things that are not real

illusion (ih-LOO-zhuhn)—a deceiving or misleading image

noblewoman (NOH-buhl-wum-uhn)—a woman of a high social class

persecution (pur-suh-KYOO-shuhn)—the act of continually treating someone cruelly and unfairly

prolific (proh-LIF-ik)—producing a large amount of something

ritual (RICH-oo-uhl)—a series of actions performed in a ceremonial order

skeptic (SKEP-tik)—someone who doubts or questions beliefs

summon (SUHM-uhn)—to call upon or send for

torture (TOR-chur)—to cause someone extreme pain or mental suffering as a punishment or as a way of forcing the person to do or say something

Troxler Effect (TRAHKS-ler i-FEKT)—an optical illusion where, by focusing on a fixed point, an object that is not the focus point begins to fade away

victim (VIK-tuhm)—a person who is hurt, killed, or made to suffer

READ MORE

Hoena, Blake. *Creepy Urban Legends*. Ghosts and Hauntings. North Mankato, MN: Capstone Press, 2018.

Kovacs, Vic. *Haunted Towns and Villages*. Haunted or Hoax? New York: Crabtree Publishing Company, 2018.

Loh-Hagan, Virginia. *Bloody Mary*. Urban Legends: Don't Read Alone! Ann Arbor, MI: Cherry Lake Publishing, 2018.

INTERNET SITES

Mirrors and Bloody Mary:
http://mentalfloss.com/article/558091/origin-bloody-mary-and-why-we-think-we-see-things-mirrors

Elizabeth Báthory's Castle:
https://www.atlasobscura.com/places/ruins-cachtice-castle

Ghost-Detecting Equipment:
https://science.howstuffworks.com/science-vs-myth/afterlife/ghost-buster4.htm

INDEX